The Mysteries of Fishing and Flight

The Mysteries of Fishing and Flight

Jacqueline K. Powers

THE POETRY PRESS
Hollywood, California

Published by
THE POETRY PRESS
of Press Americana

the press of

Americana:
The Institute for the Study of
American Popular Culture
7095-1240 Hollywood Boulevard
Hollywood, CA 90028

http://www.americanpopularculture.com

Note on Cover Art: Detail from David Farquharson's *The End of the Day's Fishing*, 1879-1885, public domain

Library of Congress Cataloging-in-Publication Data

Powers, Jacqueline K.
The mysteries of fishing and flight / Jacqueline K. Powers.
p. cm.
Includes bibliographical references.
ISBN 978-0-9829558-2-6
I. Title.
PS3616.O88345M97 2011
811'.6--dc23
2011033208

the other bird came back and they both
circled, looking perhaps for a draft;
they turned a few more times, possibly
rising – at least, clearly resting –
then flew on falling into distance till
they broke across the local bush and
trees: it was a sight of bountiful
majesty and integrity: the having
patterns and routes, breaking
from them to explore other patterns or
better ways to routes, and then the
return: a dance sacred as the sap in
the trees, permanent in its descriptions
as the ripples round the brook's
ripplestone: fresh as this particular
flood of burn breaking across us now
from the sun.

– A.R. Ammons, "Easter Morning"

Table of Contents

The Mysteries of Fishing and Flight

Back then it was late afternoon.
At least it always felt like late afternoon,
rich with plummy odors of wine and regret.
For years I tugged and thrashed
like a trout on the line in an effort to break free.
Days cascaded, eddied into deep
drifted pools. From a great distance, flashes
of silver and shade. Or a dream. Still,
no harboring silence, no safe flight.
It was my habit to sit in another room,
just beyond the pallid sweep of light,
the demarcation on the oak floor. Even then
I understood it was my choice, if such
a small act could be called a choice.
If such a small choice could be called
anything at all. Perhaps I hear
my daughter's voice as I pour another glass
of wine. As I watch night drift like smoke
into the room. When all regrets
have been pondered, small lies retold.
An angelus, my daughter's voice. I wonder,
she asks: what is the precise density
required for flight? Now, encountering you
in the hallway as if a stranger,
or sitting in a soft swell of light absorbed
in matters close at hand, or perhaps far-flung
and other worldly, I feel a frisson of shock,
of unexpected pleasure so pure I have to
step away or fall. You were always there,
waiting for me to untangle myself.
To set my own snarled dragline free.

Alone

Despite or because –
not an island, exactly, though
you say I live too much inside myself.
Perhaps a peninsula,
a cautious jutting forth.

We watch a speckled fawn
under the apple tree, feet splayed.
A hummingbird's
rapid-fire assaults on red plastic.

Gymnastic squirrels
inadvertently shake birdseed
to the ground and a trio of wild turkeys,
the painted tuft
of a red-crested lucy bird.

Silence like waves through water –
then humid-heavy birdsong.
Later a full moon, garish
as a clown's face
but I can just about breathe again.

Chaos Theory

Through a window
glazed with rain, red buds.
On the corner
an inside-out umbrella unfurls like a sail.
Wind and sand glaze the panes.
Somewhere a song.
Somewhere, the sharp scent of pines.
Still, you sleep.

Saturday Afternoon in the Garden

The shape of things, ephemeral –
curve of an arc here, straight line there.
Contrails exhaust jet plumes.
Sky's the limit but
we're already heavy on the downside.

Easy to pretend
we know which tail wags.
Moss grows on the north side of trees,
constellations fly by night.
Weeds begrudge every browned out inch
and bleeding heart, columbine.

Some days don't stand a chance.
A voice raised here, door slammed there.
Kids done, gone
these sun-down daisy chain days.

Maybe we can pick patio furniture
without a fight – maybe not.
Thirty-three years later and still fresh ice
breaks through
or a wind-hot breath licks my neck.

It's a matter of survival – the lock-step
stutter start-stop
of two minds clinging, clanging
no matter what truths remain unspoken.
Somewhere it's written on a wall.

Easter Morning

This is no bird-dappled Easter Morning,
sunstruck, no, just you and me staring,
and an empty house,
those colored egg dream kids
climbing trees, throwing sticks and stones,
some broken bones gone now,
the occasional half-drunk hilarity
has faded, and I wonder, did we stand
or did we fail, or does it not matter
in any case, now that our time
has come and (perhaps) gone,
and you on the floor
on your side in the kitchen,
fingers twitching,
plates and dishes scattered, ambulance
and sirens rushing, wailing,
a corpus wired for sound, bleep-blips,
red/green lights flashing
a silent prayer, a rosary of sorts,
though it's not time,
there's time enough yet for all that
and more, but this Easter Morning
we will make our own way,
unfettered, unbound,
search out wild orchids in the shadowed
crotch of chilly trees, forsythia
in a jelly jar, abundant, and spring rain,
while in the pond
a thousand fish waiting to be born.

Crows

In the bare branches
loneliness perches like crows.
Sometimes at night
I can hear the lake freeze.
Sometimes I can't find your light
in my dark.
Outside rose petals fall like rain.
Sometimes I dream
I can fly.

The Miracle of Jean's Rose

Her body is fragile as old porcelain
but never still –
its constant motion involuntary,
as though her neurons are trying
to outrun time.

We both try to ignore it,
sip cinnamon tea at her plastic table.
The table is covered
with an embroidered cloth
now dingy, threadbare
but each stitch straight, even hopeful.

The house smells of cat pee.
Her hand trembles – I wait for the tea
to spill or her hand
to make it to her mouth, wonder
which will come first.

The candles like old shoes worn
at the heels, but not ready
to be replaced
still good for cobweb corners,
horsehair sofas.

The waitress at the diner calls her *hon –
Hihonhowyadoinhon?*
I want to smack her
but then the stack
of egg-crusted plates would crash
and after all she's only doing her job,
maybe thinking of her next cigarette.

Jean has breakfast at the diner
every Sunday after church –
still sings in the choir, a new
trill to her soprano.

Every week someone else has passed,
another funeral, another name
to add to the list.
Over a bowl of Cream of Wheat
she says she wants to be cremated.
I ask where she wants her ashes spread
and she shrugs –
I don't know, someplace nice, she says.

I tell her I'll spread her ashes on my garden.
It will be winter,
but soon a white rose will grow
through the hard dirt and snow.
Crowds will come from across
the land to see the virgin's face in the white rose –
the miracle of Jean's rose.
Diners turn their heads when we laugh.
*It's good to know
everything will be gone but nothing lost,* she says.

Geography of a Soul

They say the dead return
to collect their footprints.
In this dry Sonora sand,
a saguaro blossom turns over
in the wind, light as
milkweed, ineffable.
The sky trembles, and you.
In a gully, bleached
white skull-curve, a bend
in time's trajectory.
The sun beats like a waiting heart.
A hawk startles, lofts, proof
the shape of the world
is the exact diameter of a single
soul, and as unknowable.

A Treatise on Religion and Finches

Through the glass door,
an invitation, or a summons.
The red brick chapel holds
no special promise,
but a bold black spire pierces
gray flannel.

Today, light pours through
a hole in the sky,
through dried leaves,
umber, bent trees.
Sharp clear scent of pine
separates every particle,

deconstructs each
beat, each thought. Hollow,
that's the word, the peculiar
shape of things, though
two yellow finches
fly past in tight-twisted

circles, chattering, oblivious
to our separate planes.
As though they hear into
this silence. As though they know
exactly where they are going,
what it will take to get there.

At the Bedside of the Eternal Matriarch

Her last breath was the same as her first,
hard and grasping. And in between
was hard, too, with no childhood
to speak of, eldest of fourteen
except one died a baby,
scarlet fever they said.
Mother's little helper and
school in jealous fits and starts before
the glove factory assembly line
and row house in Philly
with her own 2.5 children, black and white
linoleum floor. How we hated
that sauerbraten smell, castor oil swill spill.
But that was later.

That was just the way things were then,
they shared what they had
slept four to a bed
and we didn't know no different back then
she always said, smiling, shaking her head.
We didn't have nuthin' but we had enough, she said.

These were spare-strong people.
Her daddy was born old. His eyes
lived somewhere else, as if long deprived of choice
hands bent like a pretzel.
He hardly ever spoke out loud.
Her momma never spoke at all, but
worked the earth with egg shells
and coffee grounds,
birthing roses big as cabbages.

In the end her face an intaglio
white cold marbled stone –
an effigy of itself.

The Precise Nature of Doubt

We are told each thing is different.
No two fallen leaves are alike,
each its own intricate, fragile design.

Perhaps precision is chaos, frozen
in the moment, the larger picture
infinite, untenable as time,

though there is no question of god
in this house. Despite all claims
to the contrary, we refuse to make pacts

with the dead. Instead we listen
to the sound rain makes as it falls
into a thirsty well. And when

night fades, the earth breathes,
and a lily blooms beneath your feet.
They say each thing

is different, yet each mind trembles
in bright stillness, each heart
a hungry mouth waiting to be filled.

Ancient History

The lake an exhalation,
gray on gray, plump and lumpy
as a comforter
worn too thin.
No sun, just a dying sky
and ice laced around the edges, brittle
as yesterday.
Where those old photos
came from, more bleached now
than black and white.
Just the two of us bright as new pennies.
Who knew how that eager light
would tarnish, and too soon?
For you, each
series of small failures, or a failure
to flourish.
What else didn't I see?
Soon the sky, the lake empties.
The sun always just beyond reach.

Celebrating 35 Years, and Lake Placid

A monsoon drove us north –
loons, hail, radio wailin'.
Later that other kind of light,
sun-blistered rain, a cold wind.

The cottage leaned out over the lake
like it wanted to dive in –
and us with it, our rockers
and books, bare calloused feet,

just a three-leg table
between us, overlapping wine rings.
Two bare-eyed window-walls
swallowed a sky

so turbulent it was almost purple,
mountains stunned into silence.
Yellow rain-slicked fishermen
hunkered down,

oars drifting,
flying fish like small submarines
or so we imagined
over candlelight, beneath a chandelier

where moose and bobcats
chase each other
and pseudo gas-fire flames
until the end of time

or thirty-five years,
whichever comes first. You and I
like separate branches of the same tree
and still counting.

Down the Shore

I.

It's raining and the rain smells of grass
as it pounds on glass doors and the rain
and grass smell the same in the dark,
same as your fingers after they've been in me,
same as fish fresh from the surf,
slip-flopping on the deck,
the way we slide together sometimes,
sheets unfurled as a mainsail.
And I imagine the surf as it was back then,
almost a song, the wind whistling
through dune grass, scattering insects,
settling into the hot, dry sand.

II.

By day the mothers lay in rows,
watching over us, watching each other
watch kids scuttling over sand,
our skin stained, soft
as a ripe peach.
The fathers and uncles
trekked each night to the taproom
up the road, drinking beer and shots,
shooting shuffleboard,
sometimes each other.
In the turgid nights mosquitoes
drowned out shouts, even whispers.
In the distance thunder, and the sea.

III.

Only white sand, crushed shells
sharp bones of bleached fish.
Cypress trees twist in the wind.
A can clatters down a gravel drive.
Fish float down the street belly-up,
bloated, one pale eye wide,
glaring, angry at my intrusion.
Doors bang open behind empty houses.
Pilings topple like pick-up stix.
My toes curl in cold, wet sand.

Dirty Dishes in Moonlight

White pines feather the mountain,
peaks fade into that other space.
Sky so fragile it cannot contain us.

A single leaf ricochets in silent
soft swelling creek dreams.
That first spring breath

through the kitchen window.
Your face washed light, curdled cream.
In the sink, dishes balance precariously

as art. Calder, perhaps,
rimmed in eggy umber, or
Miró, teetering on the brink: red, expectant.

Outside, moss shadows the spine of trees.
A field opens like a river. Birds.
When you wake,

snow's smothering song.
One by one, footprints drift from the porch.
Again, we stumble.

A red fox skims the distance
between us. Branches, tree trunks,
frozen ground.

An abandoned barn defies gravity.
Soon a moon, big
and bright as an ocean in bloom.

Hunting With My Father

There were three of us that day – my father, the gun, and me. The ground was frozen white, the sparse woods a patchwork of dark and light. Metallic smell of snow in the air. My father placed his hand on my shoulder. We walked that way for a time. I'd lost one sodden, red mitten when we startled deer in the woods off to the right. One doe stood rooted. Stared. So did my father. The deer scattered. The doe stumbled. Fell on her side with a crash. She cried out. Her eyes were pleading and frantic at the same time. I thought she would never get up. I knocked my father's arm just as he shot. I was sure she was dead, but she crawled to her knees, then stood and limped away. A red ribbon staining the snow. My father chased her down. Said it had to be done. I still see those eyes in my dreams. In my dark. My father suddenly a stranger in the harsh white glare.

Cats and Dogs Do It Too

Excrement exists.
I don't think I need to remind you
of this but I will.

A gold lady lies naked,
discarded by the side of the road,
one lascivious leg bent beneath her,

bird shit splattered
on three painted toes
but nonetheless proud throne

for a three-legged cat
who chewed her way out
of a frozen trap one winter night,

in the process losing the tip
of her orange tail,
one frost-bitten ear

but not her nerve.
She watches now with
one red eye, wary but unconcerned.

Some nights I dream of excrement,
piles of dog shit on my best nights
but of human waste too,

filthy stalls, public spaces
no locks behind which to hide
you dirty little golden girl

naked, too, and I wonder
after Googling my dreams
what mess I am trying to extricate

myself from
what certainties
I must toss to the curb.

Continuum Mechanics

The bird feeder is empty –
deer look haggard and thin.
The first robin swallows its song,
killing the blues.
Dogs turn away in disgust, insist
on peeing on the porch.

The principle
of angular momentum balance:
If I turn one way, you turn the other.
Vector and tensor theory
expressed as doubt.

Under a thin coating of ice
yellow crocus try to sink
back into the earth
but somewhere heather is blooming
on a moor.
A strange man wearing
a blue beret smiles.

That flash –
the exact moment the sun sets over the bay
and the whole world
turns green, the tide still,
a black reminder.
No one has to sink, you say.

Thin Ice

Alone, the coyote's grizzled snout
narrow against the snow.
A shallow rib-sticking breath,
another –
and small prey schemes, decay.
The smell of fear contagious.
Human Elks

a dying breed.
Ten men in a smoke-filled room
snarf cheese balls through straws.
Miller Lite's a litmus test –
sound optional on the boob tube.
No one notices
a shadow gone. In minutes
they're my best friends.
When we leave I mourn their life way

passing.
Another species.
Shorelines erode,
continents slide off the edge,
succumb
to fractal quakes. Eco-terrorists
bomb small vineyards,
honeybees vanish from the food chain.

Bats no longer fly at night.
We become more solitary.
Or maybe
it's just the weight of particular words.
Everyone knows
it's thin ice out there –
that's why we dance so close.

At the Gym

Outside the wall of glass
snow and wind blow horizontal
a flock of starlings rises,
darts toward the far bank
before dividing, as if on cue
into two irregular black clouds.
Framed by sculpted steel, flesh

the canal freezes
in splotchy patched cubes.
She imagines oleander –
scarlet, blush,
while deep below the blank surface
a carp, almost translucent,
trapped in its own silvery arc.

Winter Morning in the Desert

Alone on foot in the dark,
far edge of the desert compound.

The path rocky, part dusty arroyo.
A palo verde tree draped

with scarlet mistletoe,
yellow barrel cactus. A startle of hawks

and a sudden thought –
of javelina, those small, hairy pigs,

their long, intrusive snouts.
Of coyotes clever enough

to send a lone female over a fence
to lure a large black dog

from the smell of yeast,
raw meat, a wood-sweet smoky fire

left unattended and fear,
implacable as a dying ember.

An Experiment in Survival Tactics

Take a breath under water, there,
take it, as if it is a living thing, a pulse.
Hold it in your hand and examine it.
Turn it over, hold it up to the light
and watch the world through it,
watch the day change color, uneasy,
black to gray to white and black again.
Oh, I know, time is no longer the failure
to act, but part of the act of action.
If only I knew which breath to take,
that one, or that. As if by choosing
I could change the way of living it,
beyond the words. Even beyond that far
swath of another soul, beckoning.

      If I turn my body toward the sky
I can breathe under water,
but in the moonlight every step I take
leads to a garden of stones.

White Dove of the Desert

As if the saguaro guards the old mission.
Inside, bones of Saint Francis. Candles
shudder, leap. Fathers and old women weep,
leach light from his bones.
As if this place holds answers.
The desert sky stretches the horizon
like a drum. Scrubbed to a new day.
As if the sand is a scourge. I long to lie
in its ashes, wear it as a second skin, gaze
through my mask at distant pines, gnarled
and misshapen as my mistakes.
As if I am nothing here, and nothing is my place.
The old woman lights her candle, bends
her broken knee.

As if there can be no god
for the people of this place, or for me.
Still, the white dove.
As if a gift.

At the Observatory Above Old San Juan

The still night air sounds heavy
with the scent of tree frogs mating
or possibly fighting, it's hard to tell
koo-keez   koo-keez.
An arc of light in the night sky.
In this place meteors, comets,
push, pull, clanging,
every ancient heart
and the deepest shadows dance
in secret-sly knowing.
Here crabs scuttle, moveable scabs
fish foul the sky, clouds,
a washbasin sea.
Hummingbirds like goldfish
goldfish the size of small cars,
or is that her imagination playing
tricks on her again?
Turtles like laundry baskets
waddle across the ashy road,
a man rides a black horse down the middle
of the street or what might
in some places be considered a street
where a rusted refrigerator
sits at a crossroads.
In this place the hot cold press of lives
against lives
soul pushing soul
today, tomorrow
yesterday a man squats
on a concrete stoop, lights a match,

nods as whole worlds burn,
as orchids tall as trees dust the rain.

How a Cypress Bends But Does Not Break

There's a tree, a Cypress I think it is,
on the island, at that point where the ocean
meets the bay. Naked, it has withstood
the tides, the winter gales and summer rains,
with exceptional grace and dexterity,
twisting and turning and bending, but moving,
always moving, so slowly
as to appear to be standing still,
an inanimate but articulate contortionist.
But standing, still.
If only we could do the same.

At Split Rock

A staircase of fossilized bones
beside a shadowed stand of white pine.
This place clings to the mountain as a mother
to her unborn child, an old woman
her faded photographs.

I listen to the silent lake, cry of the loon.
The woman's cry. The dry whisper
her tissue-paper hand makes beneath my own.
Rattle of bones like charms
on a silver bracelet she once owned.

From behind a pink plastic visor,
she cannot see the broken stones
beneath her feet.
Watch waves break across the sky.

At night she casts a solitary queen of hearts
on the deck laid out before her.
Waits for lost love
or a change in the weather.
Her teeth tread water in a glass beside her bed.

Playing with Matches

It was my mother's new Thunderbird
I drove onto a concrete divider.
Men straggled out of the bar to laugh
at it dangling there like a seesaw

then stared at me like I was home plate
but we were always some kind
of balancing act, two trains
on different tracks. In the Andes.

My mother was not the one who
made me, I'm pretty sure of that.
I don't recall smother hugs
or the soft hover of mother-breath,

though there's a brown-edged photo
of her gripping my hands at age three,
knee-deep as we both squint
into a brackish wavelet,

her hair long and starla smooth,
not gunmetal, primped into permed
submission. If giving birth is like spitting
a watermelon there were ants at this

picnic and I was always ravenous and wild.
She was from poor and needed her
2.5 TV's, her trash compactor
and no flesh-flashing mini-skirt

was going to cut her from that herd,
daughter or no daughter.
Like that day she found us playing doctor
under the front porch behind

the blackberry bush. Her haloed face
in the dim light, mouth like a knife,
the sharp sound of slaps
against bare young flesh

and then, *GOOD LITTLE GIRLS DON'T –*
Still, when I drove her to the airport
it was like I dropped into a pile of dry leaves
in autumn, ready for a match.

Feng Shui

It was a cup of coffee and throw
in another load of laundry
kind of morning,
dishes piled by the sink
like a shanty town

or dysfunctional erector set.
If that morning had a color it was pale
but it turned red fast
enough. When I caught sight of her,
arms herky jerky, shoulders

heaving, gulping
I thought she was laughing
but then that bottle of pills
dive bombing down her throat,
face awash

and came up hard against
all my misgivings
but she was *just a teen,* they said
just a gesture, they said.
That was all a long time ago

before we feng shuied ourselves
into some other serenity
martini-style.
Now she has her own dirty laundry.
Last night I dreamed

about a horse, not a well-muscled steed,
just a piebald pony
swaying to some dippity-doo
carousel tune, but still.
We ended in some place

I didn't know
and couldn't name, all sharp angles,
stairs yet another misstep.
Just trying
to find that second cup of coffee.

The Metaphysics of a Morning Run

A morning clear and cool
as a tidal pool
but my footsteps slow
as though running through
molasses. Through thick, hot tar.
Our words stones,
a rock-tangled road.
How I can never change your mind
about a single thing.
As though we are always running
in opposite directions.
There. Our shuttered door.

The Problem of Intelligent Design

This world, lacking either intelligence
or design, but offshore,
crashing waves, a tuning fork,
bending sound and spheres.
Some things are not negotiable.
This ocean is here,
whether I am away, or gone.
Here, gauze curtains surf-sing a breeze,
this simple light-line casts
no shadow, by will or desire.
Some say the world is so complex
a higher being must have fashioned it,
so as to make the magnificent mundane.
This is not science, or reason,
this longing for purpose. Across
the nation a war is raging,
newspaper headlines scream,
court cases fired like bullets, preachers
pontificate, scientists adjust
vowels, dusty bow ties, declaim.
On a sunny day the shallow tidal pool
a mirror, cosmos or chaos?
Palms sway beneath the weight
of slashing seaside rains,
and a conch shell perfectly mimics
the rushing world from which
it has been drawn, if reluctantly.
Splayed sun-loggy on the beach, your
pheromones improbably cling to mine,
both just struggling to evolve.

Ghost Notes on the Water

Today the sun is ice on the river.
We walk next to trash
trapped weeds.
Oil slicks open like rain clouds,
birds flutter in the muck.
This is your place. I feel
your breath on my face.
These buildings have no eyes.
An old man, perhaps a ghost,
whistles as he strolls by,
a wrong note.
A rucksack rides his back.
This town, now folded in upon itself,
no thought for those left behind.
Today I feel the current
of your fingers.
When I stumble,
you catch my arm. My thoughts.
Your breath lifts my hair.
The old man turns aside. Or you.

Composition: Still Life

This is no dream,
gliding across a bare wood floor.
Beat by beat,
an empty room,
yet sonorous.
It's all a matter of perspective:
the moon,
imitating itself.

That deep
refrain,
how a river bends into stillness.
There is no retreat.
We are caught
between a cello thrum
and a flute.
This is how we compose ourselves.
Like Monet:
clarity comes with distance.
Up close, a thousand brilliant daubs.

Sand Hill Cranes and Other Eccentricities

The sky bends
an egret flies.
I can almost follow.
Mossy strands
flutter-tango in the cypress grove.
Still air
hangs heavy
as I swim to river's end.
On the other side,
a dusty street.
Sand hill cranes stop.
Peer from side to side.
Eye me with disdain, or compassion.
Ignoring golf carts
and other impediments,
they stroll on.

Lilac

The huge lilac around the corner
burst out overnight, its blossoms so sweet
succulent they almost made me weep.

From my bedroom window
I can still see the empty space left
by the brontosaurus-sized lilac I attacked

three years ago for no reason I can recall,
except it had grown so wild and unruly,
its untidy ground swept branches

twisted and looped through the leaves
of an elderly apple tree, blocking my view
of the wild roses beyond – or what matters.

It seems you can cut more
than the green from things – like winter wools
and worn slippers, well-thumbed flesh.

Soon as it was done how I wanted
that lilac back, realized that showy bush
was the view of beyond. Now just a bare stump.

Jetty

As though only the idea remains.
The rocks gone, and the pools,
beneath their burden of sand,
calcified brittle bodies.
Sea urchins, slivers
of bone and shell,
silvered scales of dead fish.
Words tossed on waves.
Gulls' cries fade
and the face of a dead father,
mother still, silent,
soon nothing left to regret.
Bland spread of beach.

Dog Days

The lawn
stiff and sharp as though
angry at the hot meagerness
of things; even the sky's
horrific light.
Splayed bushes, insects, dust.
Lust laid waste.
But from this spent soil –
or some other place
of richer loam, of wet leaves,
sharp smell of rain – words,
finally, like lost art
in the telling.

Long Lake

Our room had a white iron bed
just a sink and metal pitcher,
bathroom down
the long narrow hall
gray and musty from bare feet.

Trout floppy fresh at the bar
in the village
and the Friday night Dairy Queen,
local girls with green hair
and green eye shadow, bruised lips,
their canned smiles
following campers, hikers,
men with hooks and flashy lures
stuck in their hats.

The moth-eaten grizzly bear
on the hotel front porch
jumped at each new summer kid,
pizza or no pizza –
fake blood dripping from its fangs.
Those days we ate
every piece of white bread
in the red plastic basket, butter too.

You could count on the mail boat
being late but bringing
that gallon of Gallo red, bags
of groceries, dumping oranges,
toothpaste, tampons on the dock,
rocking in its own wake.

We wrote our names on rocks,
watched them sink,
tried to find the bottom of the lake.
That cold air like pine spray,
those loons, always
a full moon drifting past.
Always the mountain had our backs.

Honeysuckle

A meadow path,
mowed between twisted
apple trees.
You pluck honeysuckle,
crush it in the palm
of your hand.

It was never my place
to find. It's only
a small patch of woods,
a place where two creeks meet,
a place where anything
seems possible,
even a red newt or two.
Everything rushes
forward here.

The sun slants steep
through pine trees, oak.
The air hums green,
thick as butter.
High glacial walls,
blue shadowed corners,

all hard edges
where sloughs of water
cut like a knife until –
finally, a shallow pool,
birthplace of a thousand
errant thoughts and
one-fisted crayfish.

I don't tell you
what I can't forget.
I don't say I feel at odds,
like a fish in a glass of water –
a turtle egg buried in sand.
I don't tell you
a weight follows me
around like a heavy wool scarf.

That I want to take off
my clothes and lie
in the creek on a bed
of sharp pebbled sand.
That maybe the cold
will clear the clutter from
inside my skin, or
maybe the dragonfly will bite.

The storm blows in fast and hard.
It rattles the rocks, stumps,
knocks down trees.
The world turns gray.
We can hardly see.
You turn toward me.
Your lips move,
and I almost hear you:
I don't want to be the one left alone.

Sign Language

This time last year not a bud in sight
but all four souls.
At least each breath,
though labored.

Now the gene pool
comes up half empty, DNA
drains away.

Still we say they are better for it.
No more slip
slide down hospital halls.
They were both ready to go

and wisteria blooms for the first time,
thick twisted rope round
a fallen tree branch,

wrecked deck.
Boards need shoring up.
Roses stunned,
frayed, heads askew.

But still, those purple flags
fly a high wind.
What's left –

the vacant space
between breaths – a sign.

Summer Squall at the Lake

It's been over a week
since they told her she has a spot
on her lung, a week
but still no word.

Sometimes rage builds slowly.
Sometimes it explodes.

Yesterday foam-froth waves
whipped the wind by the point,
white sails heeling almost horizontal.
The deer are fat and lush,
lazy as a fresh-mowed lawn.

I no longer call twice a day.
I tell myself it's an act of will.
Besides, she promised to ring.
I pretend I believe her.

Today the heat is a wet
wool blanket weighting me down,
thick curdled cream clouds low
in the sky.

Days once moved fast as a squall
crossing the lake. Now they drift,
snagged in deep cross-currents.
On the surface the lake is calm, amniotic.
Why do I feel like crying?

The phone rings.
I can't decide if I should answer.

Google says these cells multiply
and divide in an unregulated manner.
Refuse to obey the rules.
I try to imagine having nothing
to do all day but divide.

Relativity, Rain Barrels and Lies

First orange poppies floppy
as drunks, then peonies
big as pie plates –

water iris, dianthus, baby's breath.
Purple has a way of taking over.
The lawn, the flowerbeds,

a wavering line of dunes.
Each progression
measured, sure –

and you will take all summer
to finish the rain barrels,
until the hope

of rain has dried into dust.
I try to understand
the theory of relativity.

Something about a photon clock
and a moving train.
But Aristotle was wrong

about so much.
You say it doesn't matter
when things get done,

or even if they don't. I try
to recall the time
we stood ankle-deep in sand

before plunging in – a time
when everything mattered.
The grass seed

has sprouted in odd,
uneven patches. Every day
you search for patterns,

signs of life.
I ask about the rain,
the train, the clock.

Just a hot summer lie –
it's no coincidence
all the leaves have flown.

March Winds

Rain rounds our edges. Lines are blurred.
Yellow finches, doves in orchestral motion –
winging it, or just high winds?

Back then we did it under blankets,
minds blind, and lust. Bare floor splinters.
You were never someone else's
new day or unmade bed.

Lying on its side, a cement owl prays,
dead leaves a prayer shawl at its feet.
Now trillium blooms in thickened veins.

Newborn, the moon is pink.
We will dive deep as river carp sing.

Swimming Lesson

Her dress in the stiff bay breeze,
a faded calico flag.
Or a sail.
Rain clouds blew in.
The sea turned shades of gray.
It might have been a warning.
She almost never spoke.

I swam to the island.
It moved farther and farther away
but I kept moving,
arms and legs pinwheeling.
The rain made the island disappear.
The shoreline drifted,
then followed the sea.

Your yellow kayak bounced
beside me.
I rolled over, onto my back.
Drank a mouthful of rain.
Once it seemed
so important to win.
Each angry word was a race.
A false start.

I thought I saw a rainbow –
startling pink, green.
I dreamed your eyes
were blue again.
Your hair thick and brown
as a pony's tail.

She grew roses big as cabbages,
peas like a string of pearls.
I thought
about the handful of dirt
she once gave me.
Thought about sinking like stone.

Just Another Star-Free Night

It seems the stars all moved
to some boxcar town in Kansas –
corn you can drown in,
rain like thunder-falls, a giant slide.

Mold in the toes of trees.
No. Been there, done that.
Back then it was called Iowa
but that was someone else's life.

It was when he said I should be
a doctor's wife and I said
hell no, baby, I need to be.
So when my brother flipped out

called me on aluminum foil or so he said.
We rode our bikes
through gritty crotch valleys
that spawned green humps, leaves,

a two-man tent in a firefight,
lightning like Fourth of July star-clusters.
I tried to explain. I am not a body
of water though, that thought.

The smooth surface of it.
Glass, then layers of dark sediment
you try to put a ribbon around –
until you reach the flesh of things.

Acknowledgments

Special thanks to the journals that previously published select poems from this collection:

'a·pos·tro·phe, How a Cypress Bends But Does Not Break

Arbutus, An Experiment in Survival Tactics

Blood Orange Review, Continuum Mechanics and Thin Ice

Boiling River, Honeysuckle

California Quarterly, The Mysteries of Fishing and Flight

Canwehaveourballback, Cats and Dogs Do It Too

Chronogram Magazine, Chaos Theory

The Dalhousie Review, The Precise Nature of Doubt

Iguana Review, Long Lake

Innisfree Poetry Journal, At the Bedside of the Eternal Matriarch and Easter Morning

Interrobang, Playing with Matches

Poesia, Dirty Dishes in Moonlight and Down the Shore

Kaleidowhirl, Hunting with My Father

Lunarosity, Geography of a Soul, Ghost Notes on the Water, White Dove of the Desert

Review Americana, Alone, Dog Days, Jetty, Just Another Star-Free Night, Lilac, The Miracle of Jean's Rose

Rhode Island Roads, Crows

River Walk Journal, Sand Hill Cranes and Other Eccentricities

Stone Table Review, The Problem of Intelligent Design

Trillium, At the Observatory Above Old San Juan

About the Author

Winner of Prize Americana for Poetry, *The Mysteries of Fishing and Flight* is a poetry collection, at once rich, evocative, enigmatic. Author Jacqueline K. Powers summons nature imagery and emotional experience to plumb the depths of human existence – ephemeral and difficult, but beautiful just the same. Her work has appeared in such creative writing journals as *Arbutus, California Quarterly, Innisfree Poetry Journal, Poesia*, and *Review Americana* among others. She lives in Ithaca, New York, where she works at Cornell University.